My Daily Emotions Log

THIS BOOK BELONGS TO

Choose two words from the list to describe how you feel today. Can't find your emotions there? Feel free to use other words.

I think these feelings are:

○ both positive
○ negative and positive
○ positive and negative
○ both negative

I feel this way because _____

_____

_____

_____

_____

_____

_____

_____

What can cheer you up or help you stay happy today? Draw them below.

EMOTIONS LIST

angry
annoyed
anxious
ashamed
awkward
brave
calm
cheerful
chill
confused
discouraged
disgusted
distracted
embarrassed
excited
friendly
guilty
happy
hopeful
jealous
lonely
loved
nervous
offended
scared
thoughtful
tired
uncomfortable
unsure
worried

Choose two words from the list to describe how you feel today. Can't find your emotions there? Feel free to use other words.

I think these feelings are:

○ both positive   ○ positive and negative
○ negative and positive   ○ both negative

I feel this way because_____

_____

_____

_____

_____

_____

_____

What can cheer you up or help you stay happy today? Draw them below.

EMOTIONS LIST ✓

angry
annoyed
anxious
ashamed
awkward
brave
calm
cheerful
chill
confused
discouraged
disgusted
distracted
embarrassed
excited
friendly
guilty
happy
hopeful
jealous
lonely
loved
nervous
offended
scared
thoughtful
tired
uncomfortable
unsure
worried

Choose two words from the list to describe how you feel today. Can't find your emotions there? Feel free to use other words.

I think these feelings are:

○ both positive   ○ positive and negative
○ negative and positive   ○ both negative

I feel this way because _____

_____

_____

_____

_____

_____

_____

_____

What can cheer you up or help you stay happy today? Draw them below.

EMOTIONS LIST

angry
annoyed
anxious
ashamed
awkward
brave
calm
cheerful
chill
confused
discouraged
disgusted
distracted
embarrassed
excited
friendly
guilty
happy
hopeful
jealous
lonely
loved
nervous
offended
scared
thoughtful
tired
uncomfortable
unsure
worried

Choose two words from the list to describe how you feel today. Can't find your emotions there? Feel free to use other words.

I think these feelings are:

○ both positive   ○ positive and negative
○ negative and positive ○ both negative

I feel this way because _____

_____

_____

_____

_____

_____

_____

_____

What can cheer you up or help you stay happy today? Draw them below.

EMOTIONS LIST ✓

angry
annoyed
anxious
ashamed
awkward
brave
calm
cheerful
chill
confused
discouraged
disgusted
distracted
embarrassed
excited
friendly
guilty
happy
hopeful
jealous
lonely
loved
nervous
offended
scared
thoughtful
tired
uncomfortable
unsure
worried

Choose two words from the list to describe how you feel today. Can't find your emotions there? Feel free to use other words.

I think these feelings are:

- ○ both positive
- ○ negative and positive
- ○ positive and negative
- ○ both negative

I feel this way because _____

_____
_____
_____
_____
_____
_____
_____

What can cheer you up or help you stay happy today? Draw them below.

EMOTIONS LIST ✓

angry
annoyed
anxious
ashamed
awkward
brave
calm
cheerful
chill
confused
discouraged
disgusted
distracted
embarrassed
excited
friendly
guilty
happy
hopeful
jealous
lonely
loved
nervous
offended
scared
thoughtful
tired
uncomfortable
unsure
worried

Choose two words from the list to describe how you feel today. Can't find your emotions there? Feel free to use other words.

I think these feelings are:

○ both positive   ○ positive and negative
○ negative and positive ○ both negative

I feel this way because_____
_____
_____
_____
_____
_____
_____
_____

What can cheer you up or help you stay happy today? Draw them below.

EMOTIONS LIST ✓

angry
annoyed
anxious
ashamed
awkward
brave
calm
cheerful
chill
confused
discouraged
disgusted
distracted
embarrassed
excited
friendly
guilty
happy
hopeful
jealous
lonely
loved
nervous
offended
scared
thoughtful
tired
uncomfortable
unsure
worried

Choose two words from the list to describe how you feel today. Can't find your emotions there? Feel free to use other words.

EMOTIONS LIST

I think these feelings are:

○ both positive ○ positive and negative
○ negative and positive ○ both negative

I feel this way because _____

_____

_____

_____

_____

_____

_____

_____

What can cheer you up or help you stay happy today? Draw them below.

angry
annoyed
anxious
ashamed
awkward
brave
calm
cheerful
chill
confused
discouraged
disgusted
distracted
embarrassed
excited
friendly
guilty
happy
hopeful
jealous
lonely
loved
nervous
offended
scared
thoughtful
tired
uncomfortable
unsure
worried

Choose two words from the list to describe how you feel today. Can't find your emotions there? Feel free to use other words.

I think these feelings are:

- ○ both positive
- ○ negative and positive
- ○ positive and negative
- ○ both negative

I feel this way because _____

_____

_____

_____

_____

_____

_____

_____

What can cheer you up or help you stay happy today? Draw them below.

EMOTIONS LIST ✓

angry
annoyed
anxious
ashamed
awkward
brave
calm
cheerful
chill
confused
discouraged
disgusted
distracted
embarrassed
excited
friendly
guilty
happy
hopeful
jealous
lonely
loved
nervous
offended
scared
thoughtful
tired
uncomfortable
unsure
worried

Choose two words from the list to describe how you feel today. Can't find your emotions there? Feel free to use other words.

I think these feelings are:

○ both positive   ○ positive and negative
○ negative and positive   ○ both negative

I feel this way because _____

_____
_____
_____
_____
_____
_____
_____

What can cheer you up or help you stay happy today? Draw them below.

EMOTIONS LIST

angry
annoyed
anxious
ashamed
awkward
brave
calm
cheerful
chill
confused
discouraged
disgusted
distracted
embarrassed
excited
friendly
guilty
happy
hopeful
jealous
lonely
loved
nervous
offended
scared
thoughtful
tired
uncomfortable
unsure
worried

Choose two words from the list to describe how you feel today. Can't find your emotions there? Feel free to use other words.

I think these feelings are:

○ both positive
○ negative and positive
○ positive and negative
○ both negative

I feel this way because _____

_____

_____

_____

_____

_____

_____

_____

What can cheer you up or help you stay happy today? Draw them below.

EMOTIONS LIST

angry
annoyed
anxious
ashamed
awkward
brave
calm
cheerful
chill
confused
discouraged
disgusted
distracted
embarrassed
excited
friendly
guilty
happy
hopeful
jealous
lonely
loved
nervous
offended
scared
thoughtful
tired
uncomfortable
unsure
worried

Choose two words from the list to describe how you feel today. Can't find your emotions there? Feel free to use other words.

I think these feelings are:

○ both positive   ○ positive and negative
○ negative and positive ○ both negative

I feel this way because_____

_____
_____
_____
_____
_____
_____
_____

What can cheer you up or help you stay happy today? Draw them below.

EMOTIONS LIST ✓

angry
annoyed
anxious
ashamed
awkward
brave
calm
cheerful
chill
confused
discouraged
disgusted
distracted
embarrassed
excited
friendly
guilty
happy
hopeful
jealous
lonely
loved
nervous
offended
scared
thoughtful
tired
uncomfortable
unsure
worried

Choose two words from the list to describe how you feel today. Can't find your emotions there? Feel free to use other words.

I think these feelings are:

○ both positive   ○ positive and negative
○ negative and positive   ○ both negative

I feel this way because_____

_____

_____

_____

_____

_____

_____

_____

What can cheer you up or help you stay happy today? Draw them below.

EMOTIONS LIST

angry
annoyed
anxious
ashamed
awkward
brave
calm
cheerful
chill
confused
discouraged
disgusted
distracted
embarrassed
excited
friendly
guilty
happy
hopeful
jealous
lonely
loved
nervous
offended
scared
thoughtful
tired
uncomfortable
unsure
worried

Choose two words from the list to describe how you feel today. Can't find your emotions there? Feel free to use other words.

I think these feelings are:

- ○ both positive
- ○ negative and positive
- ○ positive and negative
- ○ both negative

I feel this way because_____

_____

_____

_____

_____

_____

_____

_____

EMOTIONS LIST

angry
annoyed
anxious
ashamed
awkward
brave
calm
cheerful
chill
confused
discouraged
disgusted
distracted
embarrassed
excited
friendly
guilty
happy
hopeful
jealous
lonely
loved
nervous
offended
scared
thoughtful
tired
uncomfortable
unsure
worried

What can cheer you up or help you stay happy today? Draw them below.

Choose two words from the list to describe how you feel today. Can't find your emotions there? Feel free to use other words.

I think these feelings are:

○ both positive   ○ positive and negative
○ negative and positive ○ both negative

I feel this way because _____

_____
_____
_____
_____
_____
_____
_____

What can cheer you up or help you stay happy today? Draw them below.

Choose two words from the list to describe how you feel today. Can't find your emotions there? Feel free to use other words.

I think these feelings are:

- ○ both positive
- ○ negative and positive
- ○ positive and negative
- ○ both negative

I feel this way because _____

_____

_____

_____

_____

_____

_____

_____

What can cheer you up or help you stay happy today? Draw them below.

EMOTIONS LIST

angry
annoyed
anxious
ashamed
awkward
brave
calm
cheerful
chill
confused
discouraged
disgusted
distracted
embarrassed
excited
friendly
guilty
happy
hopeful
jealous
lonely
loved
nervous
offended
scared
thoughtful
tired
uncomfortable
unsure
worried

Choose two words from the list to describe how you feel today. Can't find your emotions there? Feel free to use other words.

I think these feelings are:

- ○ both positive
- ○ negative and positive
- ○ positive and negative
- ○ both negative

I feel this way because _____

_____

_____

_____

_____

_____

_____

_____

What can cheer you up or help you stay happy today? Draw them below.

EMOTIONS LIST ✓

angry
annoyed
anxious
ashamed
awkward
brave
calm
cheerful
chill
confused
discouraged
disgusted
distracted
embarrassed
excited
friendly
guilty
happy
hopeful
jealous
lonely
loved
nervous
offended
scared
thoughtful
tired
uncomfortable
unsure
worried

Choose two words from the list to describe how you feel today. Can't find your emotions there? Feel free to use other words.

I think these feelings are:

○ both positive   ○ positive and negative
○ negative and positive   ○ both negative

I feel this way because_____

_____
_____
_____
_____
_____
_____
_____

What can cheer you up or help you stay happy today? Draw them below.

EMOTIONS LIST ✓

angry
annoyed
anxious
ashamed
awkward
brave
calm
cheerful
chill
confused
discouraged
disgusted
distracted
embarrassed
excited
friendly
guilty
happy
hopeful
jealous
lonely
loved
nervous
offended
scared
thoughtful
tired
uncomfortable
unsure
worried

Choose two words from the list to describe how you feel today. Can't find your emotions there? Feel free to use other words.

I think these feelings are:

○ both positive ○ positive and negative
○ negative and positive ○ both negative

I feel this way because_____

_____

_____

_____

_____

_____

_____

_____

What can cheer you up or help you stay happy today? Draw them below.

EMOTIONS LIST ✓

angry
annoyed
anxious
ashamed
awkward
brave
calm
cheerful
chill
confused
discouraged
disgusted
distracted
embarrassed
excited
friendly
guilty
happy
hopeful
jealous
lonely
loved
nervous
offended
scared
thoughtful
tired
uncomfortable
unsure
worried

Choose two words from the list to describe how you feel today. Can't find your emotions there? Feel free to use other words.

I think these feelings are:

○ both positive   ○ positive and negative
○ negative and positive   ○ both negative

I feel this way because _____

_____

_____

_____

_____

_____

_____

_____

What can cheer you up or help you stay happy today? Draw them below.

EMOTIONS LIST

angry
annoyed
anxious
ashamed
awkward
brave
calm
cheerful
chill
confused
discouraged
disgusted
distracted
embarrassed
excited
friendly
guilty
happy
hopeful
jealous
lonely
loved
nervous
offended
scared
thoughtful
tired
uncomfortable
unsure
worried

Choose two words from the list to describe how you feel today. Can't find your emotions there? Feel free to use other words.

I think these feelings are:

○ both positive   ○ positive and negative
○ negative and positive   ○ both negative

I feel this way because _____
_____
_____
_____
_____
_____
_____
_____

What can cheer you up or help you stay happy today? Draw them below.

EMOTIONS LIST ✓

angry
annoyed
anxious
ashamed
awkward
brave
calm
cheerful
chill
confused
discouraged
disgusted
distracted
embarrassed
excited
friendly
guilty
happy
hopeful
jealous
lonely
loved
nervous
offended
scared
thoughtful
tired
uncomfortable
unsure
worried

Choose two words from the list to describe how you feel today. Can't find your emotions there? Feel free to use other words.

I think these feelings are:

- ○ both positive
- ○ negative and positive
- ○ positive and negative
- ○ both negative

I feel this way because _____

_____

_____

_____

_____

_____

_____

_____

What can cheer you up or help you stay happy today? Draw them below.

EMOTIONS LIST ✓

angry
annoyed
anxious
ashamed
awkward
brave
calm
cheerful
chill
confused
discouraged
disgusted
distracted
embarrassed
excited
friendly
guilty
happy
hopeful
jealous
lonely
loved
nervous
offended
scared
thoughtful
tired
uncomfortable
unsure
worried

Choose two words from the list to describe how you feel today. Can't find your emotions there? Feel free to use other words.

I think these feelings are:

○ both positive   ○ positive and negative
○ negative and positive   ○ both negative

I feel this way because _____

_____
_____
_____
_____
_____
_____
_____

What can cheer you up or help you stay happy today? Draw them below.

EMOTIONS LIST ✓

angry
annoyed
anxious
ashamed
awkward
brave
calm
cheerful
chill
confused
discouraged
disgusted
distracted
embarrassed
excited
friendly
guilty
happy
hopeful
jealous
lonely
loved
nervous
offended
scared
thoughtful
tired
uncomfortable
unsure
worried

Choose two words from the list to describe how you feel today. Can't find your emotions there? Feel free to use other words.

I think these feelings are:

○ both positive   ○ positive and negative
○ negative and positive ○ both negative

I feel this way because_____

_____

_____

_____

_____

_____

_____

_____

EMOTIONS LIST

angry
annoyed
anxious
ashamed
awkward
brave
calm
cheerful
chill
confused
discouraged
disgusted
distracted
embarrassed
excited
friendly
guilty
happy
hopeful
jealous
lonely
loved
nervous
offended
scared
thoughtful
tired
uncomfortable
unsure
worried

What can cheer you up or help you stay happy today? Draw them below.

Choose two words from the list to describe how you feel today. Can't find your emotions there? Feel free to use other words.

I think these feelings are:

- ○ both positive
- ○ negative and positive
- ○ positive and negative
- ○ both negative

I feel this way because _____

_____

_____

_____

_____

_____

_____

_____

What can cheer you up or help you stay happy today? Draw them below.

EMOTIONS LIST

angry
annoyed
anxious
ashamed
awkward
brave
calm
cheerful
chill
confused
discouraged
disgusted
distracted
embarrassed
excited
friendly
guilty
happy
hopeful
jealous
lonely
loved
nervous
offended
scared
thoughtful
tired
uncomfortable
unsure
worried

Choose two words from the list to describe how you feel today. Can't find your emotions there? Feel free to use other words.

I think these feelings are:

○ both positive ○ positive and negative
○ negative and positive ○ both negative

I feel this way because_____

_____

_____

_____

_____

_____

_____

_____

What can cheer you up or help you stay happy today? Draw them below.

EMOTIONS LIST

angry
annoyed
anxious
ashamed
awkward
brave
calm
cheerful
chill
confused
discouraged
disgusted
distracted
embarrassed
excited
friendly
guilty
happy
hopeful
jealous
lonely
loved
nervous
offended
scared
thoughtful
tired
uncomfortable
unsure
worried

Choose two words from the list to describe how you feel today. Can't find your emotions there? Feel free to use other words.

I think these feelings are:

○ both positive   ○ positive and negative
○ negative and positive ○ both negative

I feel this way because_____

_____

_____

_____

_____

_____

_____

_____

What can cheer you up or help you stay happy today? Draw them below.

EMOTIONS LIST

angry
annoyed
anxious
ashamed
awkward
brave
calm
cheerful
chill
confused
discouraged
disgusted
distracted
embarrassed
excited
friendly
guilty
happy
hopeful
jealous
lonely
loved
nervous
offended
scared
thoughtful
tired
uncomfortable
unsure
worried

Choose two words from the list to describe how you feel today. Can't find your emotions there? Feel free to use other words.

I think these feelings are:

○ both positive   ○ positive and negative
○ negative and positive   ○ both negative

I feel this way because _____
_____
_____
_____
_____
_____
_____
_____

EMOTIONS LIST ✓

angry
annoyed
anxious
ashamed
awkward
brave
calm
cheerful
chill
confused
discouraged
disgusted
distracted
embarrassed
excited
friendly
guilty
happy
hopeful
jealous
lonely
loved
nervous
offended
scared
thoughtful
tired
uncomfortable
unsure
worried

What can cheer you up or help you stay happy today? Draw them below.

Choose two words from the list to describe how you feel today. Can't find your emotions there? Feel free to use other words.

I think these feelings are:

- ○ both positive
- ○ negative and positive
- ○ positive and negative
- ○ both negative

I feel this way because _____

_____

_____

_____

_____

_____

_____

_____

What can cheer you up or help you stay happy today? Draw them below.

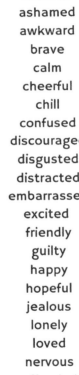

EMOTIONS LIST

angry
annoyed
anxious
ashamed
awkward
brave
calm
cheerful
chill
confused
discouraged
disgusted
distracted
embarrassed
excited
friendly
guilty
happy
hopeful
jealous
lonely
loved
nervous
offended
scared
thoughtful
tired
uncomfortable
unsure
worried

Choose two words from the list to describe how you feel today. Can't find your emotions there? Feel free to use other words.

I think these feelings are:

○ both positive   ○ positive and negative
○ negative and positive   ○ both negative

I feel this way because_____

_____

_____

_____

_____

_____

_____

_____

What can cheer you up or help you stay happy today? Draw them below.

EMOTIONS LIST

angry
annoyed
anxious
ashamed
awkward
brave
calm
cheerful
chill
confused
discouraged
disgusted
distracted
embarrassed
excited
friendly
guilty
happy
hopeful
jealous
lonely
loved
nervous
offended
scared
thoughtful
tired
uncomfortable
unsure
worried

Choose two words from the list to describe how you feel today. Can't find your emotions there? Feel free to use other words.

I think these feelings are:

○ both positive   ○ positive and negative
○ negative and positive   ○ both negative

I feel this way because _____
_____
_____
_____
_____
_____
_____
_____

What can cheer you up or help you stay happy today? Draw them below.

EMOTIONS LIST ✓

angry
annoyed
anxious
ashamed
awkward
brave
calm
cheerful
chill
confused
discouraged
disgusted
distracted
embarrassed
excited
friendly
guilty
happy
hopeful
jealous
lonely
loved
nervous
offended
scared
thoughtful
tired
uncomfortable
unsure
worried

Choose two words from the list to describe how you feel today. Can't find your emotions there? Feel free to use other words.

I think these feelings are:

○ both positive   ○ positive and negative
○ negative and positive   ○ both negative

I feel this way because_____

_____

_____

_____

_____

_____

_____

_____

What can cheer you up or help you stay happy today? Draw them below.

EMOTIONS LIST

angry
annoyed
anxious
ashamed
awkward
brave
calm
cheerful
chill
confused
discouraged
disgusted
distracted
embarrassed
excited
friendly
guilty
happy
hopeful
jealous
lonely
loved
nervous
offended
scared
thoughtful
tired
uncomfortable
unsure
worried

Choose two words from the list to describe how you feel today. Can't find your emotions there? Feel free to use other words.

I think **these feelings** are:

○ both positive   ○ positive and negative
○ negative and positive ○ both negative

I feel this way because _____

_____

_____

_____

_____

_____

_____

_____

What can cheer you up or help you stay happy today? Draw them below.

EMOTIONS LIST

angry
annoyed
anxious
ashamed
awkward
brave
calm
cheerful
chill
confused
discouraged
disgusted
distracted
embarrassed
excited
friendly
guilty
happy
hopeful
jealous
lonely
loved
nervous
offended
scared
thoughtful
tired
uncomfortable
unsure
worried

Choose two words from the list to describe how you feel today. Can't find your emotions there? Feel free to use other words.

I think these feelings are:

○ both positive   ○ positive and negative
○ negative and positive ○ both negative

I feel this way because _____

_____
_____
_____
_____
_____
_____
_____

What can cheer you up or help you stay happy today? Draw them below.

EMOTIONS LIST ✓

angry
annoyed
anxious
ashamed
awkward
brave
calm
cheerful
chill
confused
discouraged
disgusted
distracted
embarrassed
excited
friendly
guilty
happy
hopeful
jealous
lonely
loved
nervous
offended
scared
thoughtful
tired
uncomfortable
unsure
worried

Choose two words from the list to describe how you feel today. Can't find your emotions there? Feel free to use other words.

EMOTIONS LIST

I think these feelings are:

○ both positive   ○ positive and negative
○ negative and positive   ○ both negative

I feel this way because_____
_____
_____
_____
_____
_____
_____
_____

What can cheer you up or help you stay happy today? Draw them below.

angry
annoyed
anxious
ashamed
awkward
brave
calm
cheerful
chill
confused
discouraged
disgusted
distracted
embarrassed
excited
friendly
guilty
happy
hopeful
jealous
lonely
loved
nervous
offended
scared
thoughtful
tired
uncomfortable
unsure
worried

Choose two words from the list to describe how you feel today. Can't find your emotions there? Feel free to use other words.

I think these feelings are:

○ both positive ○ positive and negative
○ negative and positive ○ both negative

I feel this way because _____

_____

_____

_____

_____

_____

_____

_____

What can cheer you up or help you stay happy today? Draw them below.

EMOTIONS LIST ✓

angry
annoyed
anxious
ashamed
awkward
brave
calm
cheerful
chill
confused
discouraged
disgusted
distracted
embarrassed
excited
friendly
guilty
happy
hopeful
jealous
lonely
loved
nervous
offended
scared
thoughtful
tired
uncomfortable
unsure
worried

Choose two words from the list to describe how you feel today. Can't find your emotions there? Feel free to use other words.

I think these feelings are:

○ both positive   ○ positive and negative
○ negative and positive ○ both negative

I feel this way because _____
_____
_____
_____
_____
_____
_____
_____

What can cheer you up or help you stay happy today? Draw them below.

EMOTIONS LIST

angry
annoyed
anxious
ashamed
awkward
brave
calm
cheerful
chill
confused
discouraged
disgusted
distracted
embarrassed
excited
friendly
guilty
happy
hopeful
jealous
lonely
loved
nervous
offended
scared
thoughtful
tired
uncomfortable
unsure
worried

Choose two words from the list to describe how you feel today. Can't find your emotions there? Feel free to use other words.

I think these feelings are:

- ○ both positive
- ○ negative and positive
- ○ positive and negative
- ○ both negative

I feel this way because _____

_____

_____

_____

_____

_____

_____

_____

What can cheer you up or help you stay happy today? Draw them below.

EMOTIONS LIST ✓

angry
annoyed
anxious
ashamed
awkward
brave
calm
cheerful
chill
confused
discouraged
disgusted
distracted
embarrassed
excited
friendly
guilty
happy
hopeful
jealous
lonely
loved
nervous
offended
scared
thoughtful
tired
uncomfortable
unsure
worried

Choose two words from the list to describe how you feel today. Can't find your emotions there? Feel free to use other words.

I think these feelings are:

○ both positive   ○ positive and negative
○ negative and positive   ○ both negative

I feel this way because_____

_____

_____

_____

_____

_____

_____

_____

What can cheer you up or help you stay happy today? Draw them below.

EMOTIONS LIST ✓

angry
annoyed
anxious
ashamed
awkward
brave
calm
cheerful
chill
confused
discouraged
disgusted
distracted
embarrassed
excited
friendly
guilty
happy
hopeful
jealous
lonely
loved
nervous
offended
scared
thoughtful
tired
uncomfortable
unsure
worried

Choose two words from the list to describe how you feel today. Can't find your emotions there? Feel free to use other words.

I think these feelings are:

○ both positive   ○ positive and negative
○ negative and positive   ○ both negative

I feel this way because _____

_____

_____

_____

_____

_____

_____

_____

What can cheer you up or help you stay happy today? Draw them below.

Choose two words from the list to describe how you feel today. Can't find your emotions there? Feel free to use other words.

I think these feelings are:

○ both positive   ○ positive and negative
○ negative and positive ○ both negative

I feel this way because _____

_____
_____
_____
_____
_____
_____
_____

What can cheer you up or help you stay happy today? Draw them below.

EMOTIONS LIST ✓

angry
annoyed
anxious
ashamed
awkward
brave
calm
cheerful
chill
confused
discouraged
disgusted
distracted
embarrassed
excited
friendly
guilty
happy
hopeful
jealous
lonely
loved
nervous
offended
scared
thoughtful
tired
uncomfortable
unsure
worried

Choose two words from the list to describe how you feel today. Can't find your emotions there? Feel free to use other words.

I think these feelings are:

○ both positive   ○ positive and negative
○ negative and positive   ○ both negative

I feel this way because _____
_____
_____
_____
_____
_____
_____
_____

What can cheer you up or help you stay happy today? Draw them below.

EMOTIONS LIST

angry
annoyed
anxious
ashamed
awkward
brave
calm
cheerful
chill
confused
discouraged
disgusted
distracted
embarrassed
excited
friendly
guilty
happy
hopeful
jealous
lonely
loved
nervous
offended
scared
thoughtful
tired
uncomfortable
unsure
worried

Choose two words from the list to describe how you feel today. Can't find your emotions there? Feel free to use other words.

I think these feelings are:

- ○ both positive
- ○ negative and positive
- ○ positive and negative
- ○ both negative

I feel this way because _____

_____

_____

_____

_____

_____

_____

_____

What can cheer you up or help you stay happy today? Draw them below.

EMOTIONS LIST ✓

angry
annoyed
anxious
ashamed
awkward
brave
calm
cheerful
chill
confused
discouraged
disgusted
distracted
embarrassed
excited
friendly
guilty
happy
hopeful
jealous
lonely
loved
nervous
offended
scared
thoughtful
tired
uncomfortable
unsure
worried

Choose two words from the list to describe how you feel today. Can't find your emotions there? Feel free to use other words.

I think these feelings are:

○ both positive ○ positive and negative
○ negative and positive ○ both negative

I feel this way because_____

_____

_____

_____

_____

_____

_____

_____

EMOTIONS LIST ✓

angry
annoyed
anxious
ashamed
awkward
brave
calm
cheerful
chill
confused
discouraged
disgusted
distracted
embarrassed
excited
friendly
guilty
happy
hopeful
jealous
lonely
loved
nervous
offended
scared
thoughtful
tired
uncomfortable
unsure
worried

What can cheer you up or help you stay happy today? Draw them below.

Choose two words from the list to describe how you feel today. Can't find your emotions there? Feel free to use other words.

I think these feelings are:

○ both positive   ○ positive and negative
○ negative and positive ○ both negative

I feel this way because _____
_____
_____
_____
_____
_____
_____
_____

What can cheer you up or help you stay happy today? Draw them below.

EMOTIONS LIST

angry
annoyed
anxious
ashamed
awkward
brave
calm
cheerful
chill
confused
discouraged
disgusted
distracted
embarrassed
excited
friendly
guilty
happy
hopeful
jealous
lonely
loved
nervous
offended
scared
thoughtful
tired
uncomfortable
unsure
worried

Choose two words from the list to describe how you feel today. Can't find your emotions there? Feel free to use other words.

I think these feelings are:

○ both positive   ○ positive and negative
○ negative and positive ○ both negative

I feel this way because _____

_____

_____

_____

_____

_____

_____

_____

EMOTIONS LIST ✓

angry
annoyed
anxious
ashamed
awkward
brave
calm
cheerful
chill
confused
discouraged
disgusted
distracted
embarrassed
excited
friendly
guilty
happy
hopeful
jealous
lonely
loved
nervous
offended
scared
thoughtful
tired
uncomfortable
unsure
worried

What can cheer you up or help you stay happy today? Draw them below.

Choose two words from the list to describe how you feel today. Can't find your emotions there? Feel free to use other words.

I think these feelings are:

○ both positive ○ positive and negative
○ negative and positive ○ both negative

I feel this way because _____

_____
_____
_____
_____
_____
_____
_____

What can cheer you up or help you stay happy today? Draw them below.

EMOTIONS LIST ✓

angry
annoyed
anxious
ashamed
awkward
brave
calm
cheerful
chill
confused
discouraged
disgusted
distracted
embarrassed
excited
friendly
guilty
happy
hopeful
jealous
lonely
loved
nervous
offended
scared
thoughtful
tired
uncomfortable
unsure
worried

Choose two words from the list to describe how you feel today. Can't find your emotions there? Feel free to use other words.

I think these feelings are:

- ○ both positive
- ○ negative and positive
- ○ positive and negative
- ○ both negative

I feel this way because _____

_____

_____

_____

_____

_____

_____

What can cheer you up or help you stay happy today? Draw them below.

EMOTIONS LIST ✓

angry
annoyed
anxious
ashamed
awkward
brave
calm
cheerful
chill
confused
discouraged
disgusted
distracted
embarrassed
excited
friendly
guilty
happy
hopeful
jealous
lonely
loved
nervous
offended
scared
thoughtful
tired
uncomfortable
unsure
worried

Choose two words from the list to describe how you feel today. Can't find your emotions there? Feel free to use other words.

I think these feelings are:

○ both positive   ○ positive and negative
○ negative and positive ○ both negative

I feel this way because_____

_____

_____

_____

_____

_____

_____

_____

What can cheer you up or help you stay happy today? Draw them below.

EMOTIONS LIST

angry
annoyed
anxious
ashamed
awkward
brave
calm
cheerful
chill
confused
discouraged
disgusted
distracted
embarrassed
excited
friendly
guilty
happy
hopeful
jealous
lonely
loved
nervous
offended
scared
thoughtful
tired
uncomfortable
unsure
worried

Choose two words from the list to describe how you feel today. Can't find your emotions there? Feel free to use other words.

I think these feelings are:

○ both positive ○ positive and negative
○ negative and positive ○ both negative

I feel this way because _____
_____
_____
_____
_____
_____
_____
_____

What can cheer you up or help you stay happy today? Draw them below.

EMOTIONS LIST

angry
annoyed
anxious
ashamed
awkward
brave
calm
cheerful
chill
confused
discouraged
disgusted
distracted
embarrassed
excited
friendly
guilty
happy
hopeful
jealous
lonely
loved
nervous
offended
scared
thoughtful
tired
uncomfortable
unsure
worried

Choose two words from the list to describe how you feel today. Can't find your emotions there? Feel free to use other words.

I think these feelings are:

○ both positive   ○ positive and negative
○ negative and positive   ○ both negative

I feel this way because_____

_____

_____

_____

_____

_____

_____

_____

What can cheer you up or help you stay happy today? Draw them below.

EMOTIONS LIST ✓

angry
annoyed
anxious
ashamed
awkward
brave
calm
cheerful
chill
confused
discouraged
disgusted
distracted
embarrassed
excited
friendly
guilty
happy
hopeful
jealous
lonely
loved
nervous
offended
scared
thoughtful
tired
uncomfortable
unsure
worried

Choose two words from the list to describe how you feel today. Can't find your emotions there? Feel free to use other words.

I think these feelings are:

○ both positive   ○ positive and negative
○ negative and positive ○ both negative

I feel this way because_____

_____
_____
_____
_____
_____
_____
_____

What can cheer you up or help you stay happy today? Draw them below.

EMOTIONS LIST ✓

angry
annoyed
anxious
ashamed
awkward
brave
calm
cheerful
chill
confused
discouraged
disgusted
distracted
embarrassed
excited
friendly
guilty
happy
hopeful
jealous
lonely
loved
nervous
offended
scared
thoughtful
tired
uncomfortable
unsure
worried

Choose two words from the list to describe how you feel today. Can't find your emotions there? Feel free to use other words.

I think these feelings are:

○ both positive   ○ positive and negative
○ negative and positive   ○ both negative

I feel this way because _____

_____
_____
_____
_____
_____
_____
_____

What can cheer you up or help you stay happy today? Draw them below.

EMOTIONS LIST

angry
annoyed
anxious
ashamed
awkward
brave
calm
cheerful
chill
confused
discouraged
disgusted
distracted
embarrassed
excited
friendly
guilty
happy
hopeful
jealous
lonely
loved
nervous
offended
scared
thoughtful
tired
uncomfortable
unsure
worried

Choose two words from the list to describe how you feel today. Can't find your emotions there? Feel free to use other words.

I think these feelings are:

○ both positive   ○ positive and negative
○ negative and positive   ○ both negative

I feel this way because_____

_____
_____
_____
_____
_____
_____
_____

What can cheer you up or help you stay happy today? Draw them below.

EMOTIONS LIST

angry
annoyed
anxious
ashamed
awkward
brave
calm
cheerful
chill
confused
discouraged
disgusted
distracted
embarrassed
excited
friendly
guilty
happy
hopeful
jealous
lonely
loved
nervous
offended
scared
thoughtful
tired
uncomfortable
unsure
worried

Choose two words from the list to describe how you feel today. Can't find your emotions there? Feel free to use other words.

I think these feelings are:

○ both positive   ○ positive and negative
○ negative and positive   ○ both negative

I feel this way because _____

_____

_____

_____

_____

_____

_____

_____

EMOTIONS LIST

angry
annoyed
anxious
ashamed
awkward
brave
calm
cheerful
chill
confused
discouraged
disgusted
distracted
embarrassed
excited
friendly
guilty
happy
hopeful
jealous
lonely
loved
nervous
offended
scared
thoughtful
tired
uncomfortable
unsure
worried

What can cheer you up or help you stay happy today? Draw them below.

Choose two words from the list to describe how you feel today. Can't find your emotions there? Feel free to use other words.

I think these feelings are:

○ both positive ○ positive and negative
○ negative and positive ○ both negative

I feel this way because _____

_____

_____

_____

_____

_____

_____

_____

EMOTIONS LIST ✓

angry
annoyed
anxious
ashamed
awkward
brave
calm
cheerful
chill
confused
discouraged
disgusted
distracted
embarrassed
excited
friendly
guilty
happy
hopeful
jealous
lonely
loved
nervous
offended
scared
thoughtful
tired
uncomfortable
unsure
worried

What can cheer you up or help you stay happy today? Draw them below.

Choose two words from the list to describe how you feel today. Can't find your emotions there? Feel free to use other words.

I think these feelings are:

○ both positive   ○ positive and negative
○ negative and positive ○ both negative

I feel this way because _____
_____
_____
_____
_____
_____
_____
_____

What can cheer you up or help you stay happy today? Draw them below.

EMOTIONS LIST ✓

angry
annoyed
anxious
ashamed
awkward
brave
calm
cheerful
chill
confused
discouraged
disgusted
distracted
embarrassed
excited
friendly
guilty
happy
hopeful
jealous
lonely
loved
nervous
offended
scared
thoughtful
tired
uncomfortable
unsure
worried

Choose two words from the list to describe how you feel today. Can't find your emotions there? Feel free to use other words.

I think these feelings are:

○ both positive   ○ positive and negative
○ negative and positive   ○ both negative

I feel this way because_____

_____

_____

_____

_____

_____

_____

_____

What can cheer you up or help you stay happy today? Draw them below.

EMOTIONS LIST ✓

angry
annoyed
anxious
ashamed
awkward
brave
calm
cheerful
chill
confused
discouraged
disgusted
distracted
embarrassed
excited
friendly
guilty
happy
hopeful
jealous
lonely
loved
nervous
offended
scared
thoughtful
tired
uncomfortable
unsure
worried

Choose two words from the list to describe how you feel today. Can't find your emotions there? Feel free to use other words.

EMOTIONS LIST

I think these feelings are:

○ both positive ○ positive and negative
○ negative and positive ○ both negative

I feel this way because_____

_____

_____

_____

_____

_____

_____

_____

What can cheer you up or help you stay happy today? Draw them below.

angry
annoyed
anxious
ashamed
awkward
brave
calm
cheerful
chill
confused
discouraged
disgusted
distracted
embarrassed
excited
friendly
guilty
happy
hopeful
jealous
lonely
loved
nervous
offended
scared
thoughtful
tired
uncomfortable
unsure
worried

Choose two words from the list to describe how you feel today. Can't find your emotions there? Feel free to use other words.

I think these feelings are:

○ both positive ○ positive and negative
○ negative and positive ○ both negative

I feel this way because_____
_____
_____
_____
_____
_____
_____
_____

What can cheer you up or help you stay happy today? Draw them below.

EMOTIONS LIST ✓

angry
annoyed
anxious
ashamed
awkward
brave
calm
cheerful
chill
confused
discouraged
disgusted
distracted
embarrassed
excited
friendly
guilty
happy
hopeful
jealous
lonely
loved
nervous
offended
scared
thoughtful
tired
uncomfortable
unsure
worried

Choose two words from the list to describe how you feel today. Can't find your emotions there? Feel free to use other words.

I think these feelings are:

○ both positive   ○ positive and negative
○ negative and positive   ○ both negative

I feel this way because_____

_____
_____
_____
_____
_____
_____
_____

What can cheer you up or help you stay happy today? Draw them below.

EMOTIONS LIST ✓

angry
annoyed
anxious
ashamed
awkward
brave
calm
cheerful
chill
confused
discouraged
disgusted
distracted
embarrassed
excited
friendly
guilty
happy
hopeful
jealous
lonely
loved
nervous
offended
scared
thoughtful
tired
uncomfortable
unsure
worried

Choose two words from the list to describe how you feel today. Can't find your emotions there? Feel free to use other words.

I think these feelings are:

○ both positive   ○ positive and negative
○ negative and positive ○ both negative

I feel this way because _____
_____
_____
_____
_____
_____
_____
_____
_____

What can cheer you up or help you stay happy today? Draw them below.

EMOTIONS LIST

angry
annoyed
anxious
ashamed
awkward
brave
calm
cheerful
chill
confused
discouraged
disgusted
distracted
embarrassed
excited
friendly
guilty
happy
hopeful
jealous
lonely
loved
nervous
offended
scared
thoughtful
tired
uncomfortable
unsure
worried

Choose two words from the list to describe how you feel today. Can't find your emotions there? Feel free to use other words.

I think **these feelings** are:

○ both positive   ○ positive and negative
○ negative and positive   ○ both negative

I feel this way because_____

_____

_____

_____

_____

_____

_____

What can cheer you up or help you stay happy today? Draw them below.

EMOTIONS LIST ✓

angry
annoyed
anxious
ashamed
awkward
brave
calm
cheerful
chill
confused
discouraged
disgusted
distracted
embarrassed
excited
friendly
guilty
happy
hopeful
jealous
lonely
loved
nervous
offended
scared
thoughtful
tired
uncomfortable
unsure
worried

Choose two words from the list to describe how you feel today. Can't find your emotions there? Feel free to use other words.

I think these feelings are:

○ both positive   ○ positive and negative
○ negative and positive   ○ both negative

I feel this way because _____

_____

_____

_____

_____

_____

_____

_____

What can cheer you up or help you stay happy today? Draw them below.

EMOTIONS LIST

angry
annoyed
anxious
ashamed
awkward
brave
calm
cheerful
chill
confused
discouraged
disgusted
distracted
embarrassed
excited
friendly
guilty
happy
hopeful
jealous
lonely
loved
nervous
offended
scared
thoughtful
tired
uncomfortable
unsure
worried

Choose two words from the list to describe how you feel today. Can't find your emotions there? Feel free to use other words.

I think these feelings are:

○ both positive ○ positive and negative
○ negative and positive ○ both negative

I feel this way because _____

_____

_____

_____

_____

_____

_____

_____

What can cheer you up or help you stay happy today? Draw them below.

EMOTIONS LIST

angry
annoyed
anxious
ashamed
awkward
brave
calm
cheerful
chill
confused
discouraged
disgusted
distracted
embarrassed
excited
friendly
guilty
happy
hopeful
jealous
lonely
loved
nervous
offended
scared
thoughtful
tired
uncomfortable
unsure
worried

Choose two words from the list to describe how you feel today. Can't find your emotions there? Feel free to use other words.

I think these feelings are:

- ○ both positive
- ○ positive and negative
- ○ negative and positive
- ○ both negative

I feel this way because _____

_____

_____

_____

_____

_____

_____

_____

What can cheer you up or help you stay happy today? Draw them below.

EMOTIONS LIST ✓

angry
annoyed
anxious
ashamed
awkward
brave
calm
cheerful
chill
confused
discouraged
disgusted
distracted
embarrassed
excited
friendly
guilty
happy
hopeful
jealous
lonely
loved
nervous
offended
scared
thoughtful
tired
uncomfortable
unsure
worried

Choose two words from the list to describe how you feel today. Can't find your emotions there? Feel free to use other words.

I think these feelings are:

○ both positive   ○ positive and negative
○ negative and positive   ○ both negative

I feel this way because _____

_____

_____

_____

_____

_____

_____

_____

What can cheer you up or help you stay happy today? Draw them below.

EMOTIONS LIST ✓

angry
annoyed
anxious
ashamed
awkward
brave
calm
cheerful
chill
confused
discouraged
disgusted
distracted
embarrassed
excited
friendly
guilty
happy
hopeful
jealous
lonely
loved
nervous
offended
scared
thoughtful
tired
uncomfortable
unsure
worried

Choose two words from the list to describe how you feel today. Can't find your emotions there? Feel free to use other words.

I think these feelings are:

○ both positive   ○ positive and negative
○ negative and positive ○ both negative

I feel this way because _____

_____

_____

_____

_____

_____

_____

_____

EMOTIONS LIST

angry
annoyed
anxious
ashamed
awkward
brave
calm
cheerful
chill
confused
discouraged
disgusted
distracted
embarrassed
excited
friendly
guilty
happy
hopeful
jealous
lonely
loved
nervous
offended
scared
thoughtful
tired
uncomfortable
unsure
worried

What can cheer you up or help you stay happy today? Draw them below.

Choose two words from the list to describe how you feel today. Can't find your emotions there? Feel free to use other words.

I think these feelings are:

○ both positive   ○ positive and negative
○ negative and positive   ○ both negative

I feel this way because _____
_____
_____
_____
_____
_____
_____
_____
_____

What can cheer you up or help you stay happy today? Draw them below.

EMOTIONS LIST

angry
annoyed
anxious
ashamed
awkward
brave
calm
cheerful
chill
confused
discouraged
disgusted
distracted
embarrassed
excited
friendly
guilty
happy
hopeful
jealous
lonely
loved
nervous
offended
scared
thoughtful
tired
uncomfortable
unsure
worried

Choose two words from the list to describe how you feel today. Can't find your emotions there? Feel free to use other words.

I think these feelings are:

- ○ both positive
- ○ negative and positive
- ○ positive and negative
- ○ both negative

I feel this way because _____

_____

_____

_____

_____

_____

_____

_____

What can cheer you up or help you stay happy today? Draw them below.

EMOTIONS LIST ✓

angry
annoyed
anxious
ashamed
awkward
brave
calm
cheerful
chill
confused
discouraged
disgusted
distracted
embarrassed
excited
friendly
guilty
happy
hopeful
jealous
lonely
loved
nervous
offended
scared
thoughtful
tired
uncomfortable
unsure
worried

Choose two words from the list to describe how you feel today. Can't find your emotions there? Feel free to use other words.

I think these feelings are:

- ○ both positive
- ○ negative and positive
- ○ positive and negative
- ○ both negative

I feel this way because _____

_____

_____

_____

_____

_____

_____

_____

What can cheer you up or help you stay happy today? Draw them below.

EMOTIONS LIST ✓

angry
annoyed
anxious
ashamed
awkward
brave
calm
cheerful
chill
confused
discouraged
disgusted
distracted
embarrassed
excited
friendly
guilty
happy
hopeful
jealous
lonely
loved
nervous
offended
scared
thoughtful
tired
uncomfortable
unsure
worried

Choose two words from the list to describe how you feel today. Can't find your emotions there? Feel free to use other words.

I think these feelings are:

○ both positive   ○ positive and negative
○ negative and positive ○ both negative

I feel this way because _____

_____

_____

_____

_____

_____

_____

_____

What can cheer you up or help you stay happy today? Draw them below.

EMOTIONS LIST ✓

angry
annoyed
anxious
ashamed
awkward
brave
calm
cheerful
chill
confused
discouraged
disgusted
distracted
embarrassed
excited
friendly
guilty
happy
hopeful
jealous
lonely
loved
nervous
offended
scared
thoughtful
tired
uncomfortable
unsure
worried

Choose two words from the list to describe how you feel today. Can't find your emotions there? Feel free to use other words.

I think these feelings are:

○ both positive ○ positive and negative
○ negative and positive ○ both negative

I feel this way because _____

_____

_____

_____

_____

_____

_____

_____

What can cheer you up or help you stay happy today? Draw them below.

EMOTIONS LIST

angry
annoyed
anxious
ashamed
awkward
brave
calm
cheerful
chill
confused
discouraged
disgusted
distracted
embarrassed
excited
friendly
guilty
happy
hopeful
jealous
lonely
loved
nervous
offended
scared
thoughtful
tired
uncomfortable
unsure
worried

Choose two words from the list to describe how you feel today. Can't find your emotions there? Feel free to use other words.

I think these feelings are:

○ both positive   ○ positive and negative
○ negative and positive   ○ both negative

I feel this way because _____

_____

_____

_____

_____

_____

_____

_____

What can cheer you up or help you stay happy today? Draw them below.

EMOTIONS LIST

angry
annoyed
anxious
ashamed
awkward
brave
calm
cheerful
chill
confused
discouraged
disgusted
distracted
embarrassed
excited
friendly
guilty
happy
hopeful
jealous
lonely
loved
nervous
offended
scared
thoughtful
tired
uncomfortable
unsure
worried

Choose two words from the list to describe how you feel today. Can't find your emotions there? Feel free to use other words.

I think **these feelings** are:

○ both positive   ○ positive and negative
○ negative and positive ○ both negative

I feel this way because _____
_____
_____
_____
_____
_____
_____
_____

What can cheer you up or help you stay happy today? Draw them below.

EMOTIONS LIST

angry
annoyed
anxious
ashamed
awkward
brave
calm
cheerful
chill
confused
discouraged
disgusted
distracted
embarrassed
excited
friendly
guilty
happy
hopeful
jealous
lonely
loved
nervous
offended
scared
thoughtful
tired
uncomfortable
unsure
worried

Choose two words from the list to describe how you feel today. Can't find your emotions there? Feel free to use other words.

I think these feelings are:

- ○ both positive
- ○ negative and positive
- ○ positive and negative
- ○ both negative

I feel this way because _____

_____

_____

_____

_____

_____

_____

_____

What can cheer you up or help you stay happy today? Draw them below.

EMOTIONS LIST

angry
annoyed
anxious
ashamed
awkward
brave
calm
cheerful
chill
confused
discouraged
disgusted
distracted
embarrassed
excited
friendly
guilty
happy
hopeful
jealous
lonely
loved
nervous
offended
scared
thoughtful
tired
uncomfortable
unsure
worried

Choose two words from the list to describe how you feel today. Can't find your emotions there? Feel free to use other words.

I think these feelings are:

○ both positive   ○ positive and negative
○ negative and positive   ○ both negative

I feel this way because_____

_____

_____

_____

_____

_____

_____

_____

What can cheer you up or help you stay happy today? Draw them below.

EMOTIONS LIST ✓

angry
annoyed
anxious
ashamed
awkward
brave
calm
cheerful
chill
confused
discouraged
disgusted
distracted
embarrassed
excited
friendly
guilty
happy
hopeful
jealous
lonely
loved
nervous
offended
scared
thoughtful
tired
uncomfortable
unsure
worried

Choose two words from the list to describe how you feel today. Can't find your emotions there? Feel free to use other words.

I think these feelings are:

○ both positive　　　　○ positive and negative
○ negative and positive　○ both negative

I feel this way because _____

_____
_____
_____
_____
_____
_____
_____

What can cheer you up or help you stay happy today? Draw them below.

EMOTIONS LIST

angry
annoyed
anxious
ashamed
awkward
brave
calm
cheerful
chill
confused
discouraged
disgusted
distracted
embarrassed
excited
friendly
guilty
happy
hopeful
jealous
lonely
loved
nervous
offended
scared
thoughtful
tired
uncomfortable
unsure
worried

Choose two words from the list to describe how you feel today. Can't find your emotions there? Feel free to use other words.

I think these feelings are:

○ both positive   ○ positive and negative
○ negative and positive   ○ both negative

I feel this way because _____

_____

_____

_____

_____

_____

_____

_____

What can cheer you up or help you stay happy today? Draw them below.

EMOTIONS LIST

angry
annoyed
anxious
ashamed
awkward
brave
calm
cheerful
chill
confused
discouraged
disgusted
distracted
embarrassed
excited
friendly
guilty
happy
hopeful
jealous
lonely
loved
nervous
offended
scared
thoughtful
tired
uncomfortable
unsure
worried

Choose two words from the list to describe how you feel today. Can't find your emotions there? Feel free to use other words.

I think these feelings are:

○ both positive   ○ positive and negative
○ negative and positive   ○ both negative

I feel this way because_____

_____

_____

_____

_____

_____

_____

_____

What can cheer you up or help you stay happy today? Draw them below.

EMOTIONS LIST ✔

angry
annoyed
anxious
ashamed
awkward
brave
calm
cheerful
chill
confused
discouraged
disgusted
distracted
embarrassed
excited
friendly
guilty
happy
hopeful
jealous
lonely
loved
nervous
offended
scared
thoughtful
tired
uncomfortable
unsure
worried

Choose two words from the list to describe how you feel today. Can't find your emotions there? Feel free to use other words.

I think **these feelings** are:

○ both positive   ○ positive and negative
○ negative and positive   ○ both negative

I feel this way because_____

_____

_____

_____

_____

_____

_____

What can cheer you up or help you stay happy today? Draw them below.

EMOTIONS LIST ✓

angry
annoyed
anxious
ashamed
awkward
brave
calm
cheerful
chill
confused
discouraged
disgusted
distracted
embarrassed
excited
friendly
guilty
happy
hopeful
jealous
lonely
loved
nervous
offended
scared
thoughtful
tired
uncomfortable
unsure
worried

Choose two words from the list to describe how you feel today. Can't find your emotions there? Feel free to use other words.

I think these feelings are:

○ both positive   ○ positive and negative
○ negative and positive   ○ both negative

I feel this way because _____
_____
_____
_____
_____
_____
_____
_____

EMOTIONS LIST

angry
annoyed
anxious
ashamed
awkward
brave
calm
cheerful
chill
confused
discouraged
disgusted
distracted
embarrassed
excited
friendly
guilty
happy
hopeful
jealous
lonely
loved
nervous
offended
scared
thoughtful
tired
uncomfortable
unsure
worried

What can cheer you up or help you stay happy today? Draw them below.

Choose two words from the list to describe how you feel today. Can't find your emotions there? Feel free to use other words.

I think these feelings are:

○ both positive   ○ positive and negative
○ negative and positive   ○ both negative

I feel this way because _____
_____
_____
_____
_____
_____
_____
_____

What can cheer you up or help you stay happy today? Draw them below.

EMOTIONS LIST ✓

angry
annoyed
anxious
ashamed
awkward
brave
calm
cheerful
chill
confused
discouraged
disgusted
distracted
embarrassed
excited
friendly
guilty
happy
hopeful
jealous
lonely
loved
nervous
offended
scared
thoughtful
tired
uncomfortable
unsure
worried

Choose two words from the list to describe how you feel today. Can't find your emotions there? Feel free to use other words.

I think these feelings are:

○ both positive   ○ positive and negative
○ negative and positive ○ both negative

I feel this way because _____
_____
_____
_____
_____
_____
_____
_____

What can cheer you up or help you stay happy today? Draw them below.

EMOTIONS LIST ✓

angry
annoyed
anxious
ashamed
awkward
brave
calm
cheerful
chill
confused
discouraged
disgusted
distracted
embarrassed
excited
friendly
guilty
happy
hopeful
jealous
lonely
loved
nervous
offended
scared
thoughtful
tired
uncomfortable
unsure
worried

Choose two words from the list to describe how you feel today. Can't find your emotions there? Feel free to use other words.

I think these feelings are:

○ both positive   ○ positive and negative
○ negative and positive   ○ both negative

I feel this way because_____
_____
_____
_____
_____
_____
_____
_____

What can cheer you up or help you stay happy today? Draw them below.

EMOTIONS LIST

angry
annoyed
anxious
ashamed
awkward
brave
calm
cheerful
chill
confused
discouraged
disgusted
distracted
embarrassed
excited
friendly
guilty
happy
hopeful
jealous
lonely
loved
nervous
offended
scared
thoughtful
tired
uncomfortable
unsure
worried

Choose two words from the list to describe how you feel today. Can't find your emotions there? Feel free to use other words.

I think these feelings are:

○ both positive
○ negative and positive
○ positive and negative
○ both negative

I feel this way because_____

_____

_____

_____

_____

_____

_____

_____

What can cheer you up or help you stay happy today? Draw them below.

EMOTIONS LIST

angry
annoyed
anxious
ashamed
awkward
brave
calm
cheerful
chill
confused
discouraged
disgusted
distracted
embarrassed
excited
friendly
guilty
happy
hopeful
jealous
lonely
loved
nervous
offended
scared
thoughtful
tired
uncomfortable
unsure
worried

Choose two words from the list to describe how you feel today. Can't find your emotions there? Feel free to use other words.

I think these feelings are:

○ both positive   ○ positive and negative
○ negative and positive ○ both negative

I feel this way because _____

_____

_____

_____

_____

_____

_____

_____

What can cheer you up or help you stay happy today? Draw them below.

EMOTIONS LIST ✓

angry
annoyed
anxious
ashamed
awkward
brave
calm
cheerful
chill
confused
discouraged
disgusted
distracted
embarrassed
excited
friendly
guilty
happy
hopeful
jealous
lonely
loved
nervous
offended
scared
thoughtful
tired
uncomfortable
unsure
worried

Choose two words from the list to describe how you feel today. Can't find your emotions there? Feel free to use other words.

I think these feelings are:

○ both positive   ○ positive and negative
○ negative and positive   ○ both negative

I feel this way because_____

_____

_____

_____

_____

_____

_____

_____

What can cheer you up or help you stay happy today? Draw them below.

EMOTIONS LIST

angry
annoyed
anxious
ashamed
awkward
brave
calm
cheerful
chill
confused
discouraged
disgusted
distracted
embarrassed
excited
friendly
guilty
happy
hopeful
jealous
lonely
loved
nervous
offended
scared
thoughtful
tired
uncomfortable
unsure
worried

Choose two words from the list to describe how you feel today. Can't find your emotions there? Feel free to use other words.

I think these feelings are:

○ both positive   ○ positive and negative
○ negative and positive ○ both negative

I feel this way because _____

_____
_____
_____
_____
_____
_____
_____

What can cheer you up or help you stay happy today? Draw them below.

EMOTIONS LIST ✓

angry
annoyed
anxious
ashamed
awkward
brave
calm
cheerful
chill
confused
discouraged
disgusted
distracted
embarrassed
excited
friendly
guilty
happy
hopeful
jealous
lonely
loved
nervous
offended
scared
thoughtful
tired
uncomfortable
unsure
worried

Choose two words from the list to describe how you feel today. Can't find your emotions there? Feel free to use other words.

I think these feelings are:

○ both positive   ○ positive and negative
○ negative and positive   ○ both negative

I feel this way because _____

_____

_____

_____

_____

_____

_____

_____

What can cheer you up or help you stay happy today? Draw them below.

EMOTIONS LIST

angry
annoyed
anxious
ashamed
awkward
brave
calm
cheerful
chill
confused
discouraged
disgusted
distracted
embarrassed
excited
friendly
guilty
happy
hopeful
jealous
lonely
loved
nervous
offended
scared
thoughtful
tired
uncomfortable
unsure
worried

Choose two words from the list to describe how you feel today. Can't find your emotions there? Feel free to use other words.

I think these feelings are:

○ both positive ○ positive and negative
○ negative and positive ○ both negative

I feel this way because_____
_____
_____
_____
_____
_____
_____
_____

What can cheer you up or help you stay happy today? Draw them below.

EMOTIONS LIST

angry
annoyed
anxious
ashamed
awkward
brave
calm
cheerful
chill
confused
discouraged
disgusted
distracted
embarrassed
excited
friendly
guilty
happy
hopeful
jealous
lonely
loved
nervous
offended
scared
thoughtful
tired
uncomfortable
unsure
worried

Choose two words from the list to describe how you feel today. Can't find your emotions there? Feel free to use other words.

I think these feelings are:

○ both positive   ○ positive and negative
○ negative and positive   ○ both negative

I feel this way because _____

_____

_____

_____

_____

_____

_____

_____

What can cheer you up or help you stay happy today? Draw them below.

EMOTIONS LIST ✓

angry
annoyed
anxious
ashamed
awkward
brave
calm
cheerful
chill
confused
discouraged
disgusted
distracted
embarrassed
excited
friendly
guilty
happy
hopeful
jealous
lonely
loved
nervous
offended
scared
thoughtful
tired
uncomfortable
unsure
worried

Choose two words from the list to describe how you feel today. Can't find your emotions there? Feel free to use other words.

EMOTIONS LIST

angry
annoyed
anxious
ashamed
awkward
brave
calm
cheerful
chill
confused
discouraged
disgusted
distracted
embarrassed
excited
friendly
guilty
happy
hopeful
jealous
lonely
loved
nervous
offended
scared
thoughtful
tired
uncomfortable
unsure
worried

I think these feelings are:

○ both positive   ○ positive and negative
○ negative and positive   ○ both negative

I feel this way because_____
_____
_____
_____
_____
_____
_____
_____

What can cheer you up or help you stay happy today? Draw them below.

Choose two words from the list to describe how you feel today. Can't find your emotions there? Feel free to use other words.

I think these feelings are:

○ both positive   ○ positive and negative
○ negative and positive   ○ both negative

I feel this way because _____

_____
_____
_____
_____
_____
_____
_____

What can cheer you up or help you stay happy today? Draw them below.

EMOTIONS LIST

angry
annoyed
anxious
ashamed
awkward
brave
calm
cheerful
chill
confused
discouraged
disgusted
distracted
embarrassed
excited
friendly
guilty
happy
hopeful
jealous
lonely
loved
nervous
offended
scared
thoughtful
tired
uncomfortable
unsure
worried

Choose two words from the list to describe how you feel today. Can't find your emotions there? Feel free to use other words.

I think these feelings are:

○ both positive
○ negative and positive
○ positive and negative
○ both negative

I feel this way because _____

_____

_____

_____

_____

_____

_____

_____

EMOTIONS LIST

angry
annoyed
anxious
ashamed
awkward
brave
calm
cheerful
chill
confused
discouraged
disgusted
distracted
embarrassed
excited
friendly
guilty
happy
hopeful
jealous
lonely
loved
nervous
offended
scared
thoughtful
tired
uncomfortable
unsure
worried

What can cheer you up or help you stay happy today? Draw them below.

Choose two words from the list to describe how you feel today. Can't find your emotions there? Feel free to use other words.

I think these feelings are:

○ both positive   ○ positive and negative
○ negative and positive   ○ both negative

I feel this way because _____
_____
_____
_____
_____
_____
_____
_____

What can cheer you up or help you stay happy today? Draw them below.

EMOTIONS LIST ✓

angry
annoyed
anxious
ashamed
awkward
brave
calm
cheerful
chill
confused
discouraged
disgusted
distracted
embarrassed
excited
friendly
guilty
happy
hopeful
jealous
lonely
loved
nervous
offended
scared
thoughtful
tired
uncomfortable
unsure
worried

Choose two words from the list to describe how you feel today. Can't find your emotions there? Feel free to use other words.

I think these feelings are:

○ both positive   ○ positive and negative
○ negative and positive   ○ both negative

I feel this way because _____
_____
_____
_____
_____
_____
_____
_____

What can cheer you up or help you stay happy today? Draw them below.

EMOTIONS LIST ✓

angry
annoyed
anxious
ashamed
awkward
brave
calm
cheerful
chill
confused
discouraged
disgusted
distracted
embarrassed
excited
friendly
guilty
happy
hopeful
jealous
lonely
loved
nervous
offended
scared
thoughtful
tired
uncomfortable
unsure
worried

Choose two words from the list to describe how you feel today. Can't find your emotions there? Feel free to use other words.

I think these feelings are:

○ both positive
○ negative and positive
○ positive and negative
○ both negative

I feel this way because _____

_____
_____
_____
_____
_____
_____
_____

What can cheer you up or help you stay happy today? Draw them below.

EMOTIONS LIST

angry
annoyed
anxious
ashamed
awkward
brave
calm
cheerful
chill
confused
discouraged
disgusted
distracted
embarrassed
excited
friendly
guilty
happy
hopeful
jealous
lonely
loved
nervous
offended
scared
thoughtful
tired
uncomfortable
unsure
worried

Choose two words from the list to describe how you feel today. Can't find your emotions there? Feel free to use other words.

I think these feelings are:

○ both positive   ○ positive and negative
○ negative and positive ○ both negative

I feel this way because _____
_____
_____
_____
_____
_____
_____
_____

What can cheer you up or help you stay happy today? Draw them below.

EMOTIONS LIST

angry
annoyed
anxious
ashamed
awkward
brave
calm
cheerful
chill
confused
discouraged
disgusted
distracted
embarrassed
excited
friendly
guilty
happy
hopeful
jealous
lonely
loved
nervous
offended
scared
thoughtful
tired
uncomfortable
unsure
worried

Printed in Great Britain
by Amazon

82755182R00058